Stranger
Danger

Priscilla Larson
Pictures by Melodye Rosales
and Karen Larson

Tyndale House
Publishers, Inc.
Wheaton, Illinois

Library of Congress Cataloging-in-Publication Data

Larson, Priscilla, date
  Stranger danger / Priscilla Larson.
       p.   cm.
  Summary: Uses a Christian perspective to describe how to deal with
strangers and avoid being molested.
  ISBN 0-8423-6599-0
  1. Children and strangers—Juvenile literature.   2. Child
molesting—United States—Prevention—Juvenile literature.   3. Child
molesting—Religious aspects—Christianity—Juvenile literature.
[1. Strangers.   2. Child molesting—Prevention.]   I. Larson, Karen,
1969-   . II. Title.
HQ784.S8L37   1991
362.7'6—dc20   91-65134

Ask your bookstore for other Eager Reader books:
Alfred MacDuff Is Afraid of War
Corey's Dad Drinks Too Much
Natalie Jean and the Flying Machine
Natalie Jean Goes Hog Wild
Natalie Jean and Tag-along Tessa
Natalie Jean and the Haints' Parade

Scripture verses are taken from *The Simplified Living Bible* © 1990 by KNT
Charitable Trust. All rights reserved.

Text © 1991 by Priscilla Larson
Cover illustration © 1991 by Melodye Rosales
Interior illustrations © 1991 by Karen Larson
All rights reserved
Printed in the United States of America

98 97 96 95 94 93 92 91
 9   8   7   6   5   4   3   2   1

To innocent children everywhere, who deserve every chance to grow up unharmed, unscathed, and happily wholesome; and to Wendy, who, in spite of a threatening encounter, did just that. In gratitude for her escape unhurt and for the benefit of all children, this book was written.

Contents

One

Dangerous Strangers

A stranger is someone you do not know.

Most strangers are good people. They are just like the people you know.

But a few strangers are dangerous. They have sick minds. There is something wrong with the way they think.

They like to touch children's bodies. Sometimes they hurt them.

These dangerous strangers are called child molesters.

A child molester looks just like other people. He may be very old or only a little older than you. You can't tell that he is dangerous.[1]

The child molester looks for children who are alone. He will be friendly. He wants you to go somewhere with him.

He knows you have been told, "Never go with strangers." He tries to make it sound OK for you to go with him.

God has given you a good mind. He wants you to plan so you will be safe.

When you are scared, ask the Lord to

1 The child molester can be a man or a woman. Or a boy or a girl. In this book we will just say it is a man.

help you. Then remember your protection plan. You will learn how to plan in this book.

Here are four safety rules to remember:

1. Never wander off in malls or outdoor places where no one is in charge.

2. Never talk to strangers.

3. Never accept food or presents from a stranger.

4. Never go with a stranger.

Don't be afraid, for I am with you. Do not be dismayed, for I am your God. I will strengthen you. I will help you. I will uphold you with my strong right hand.

(Isaiah 41:10)

Two

Car Tricks

The Stranger's Strategy

Sometimes a child molester drives a car. He looks for a child who is alone. He wants you to go with him. Here are some lies he uses.

"Your mother is sick. She sent me to get you."

"I can't find Main Street. Come with me. You can show me where it is. I'll give you some money and a ride home."

"You've won a contest! I'll take you to
collect your prize."

"You must be wet and cold. It's raining
so hard! Would you like to ride home in
my warm car?"

Your Protection Plan

Basic Rule: Do not accept a ride from a stranger.

   1. A stranger stops his car beside you. *Do not go near the car*. Keep walking.

2. The stranger talks to you. Say, "I cannot talk to strangers." Hurry away!

3. The stranger doesn't leave you alone. Go to a safe place nearby: a friend's home, a safe house, a school, or a store. Tell the person in charge what happened. Call your parents or the person who is taking care of you. Ask them what you should do.

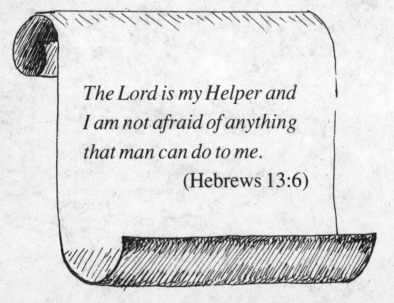

The Lord is my Helper and I am not afraid of anything that man can do to me.

(Hebrews 13:6)

Three
Playground Ploys

The Stranger's Strategy

A stranger might approach you on the playground. Here are some of his tricks.

You are swinging on a swing set. He offers to push you.

You are playing ball. He might ask to play with you.

He may say, "I have something to show you!" He will ask you to go with him.

He might try to take off your clothes.

He might try to touch your body.

Your Protection Plan

Basic Rule: Know who is in charge of the playground.

1. A stranger offers to push you on the swing. Or he asks to play ball with you. Say, "No, thank you." Go away from him.

2. A stranger hangs around and watches you. He may ask you to go with him. Don't go with him! Tell the playground supervisor. Or tell the person who is in charge of you.

3. A stranger touches you on your private parts. Say, "Don't do that!" Walk away toward people.

4. A stranger grabs you or blocks your way. Yell and make a lot of noise. Call for someone to come help you. Keep yelling until he lets you go.

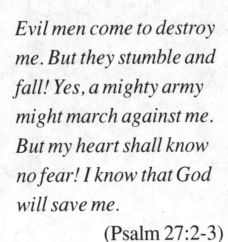

Evil men come to destroy me. But they stumble and fall! Yes, a mighty army might march against me. But my heart shall know no fear! I know that God will save me.

(Psalm 27:2-3)

Four

The Phoney on the Phone

The Stranger's Strategy

Sometimes a child molester makes phone calls. He finds someone who is home alone. Then he goes to the house. He tries to fool the child into letting him in.

Here are some tricks he uses on the phone.

He might ask to speak to one of your parents. He might ask, "Is there another adult at home?" What does he want to find out? He wants to find out if you are alone.

He might ask, "How soon do you expect someone?" What does he want to know? He wants to know how long you will be alone.

He might ask, "Does your mother work away from home?" What does he want to know? He wants to know if you are home alone often.

Your Protection Plan

Basic Rule: Do not tell a stranger that you are home alone.

1. Someone calls and asks for your parents. They aren't home. Say, "My mother can't come to the phone.

Leave your number. She will call you
back."

2. You receive a call that frightens
you. Call your mom or dad. Or call
the person you are to call in
emergencies.

3. A stranger asks if your mother works away from home. Do not tell him. Say, "You are not in our family. You do not need to know."

4. Put these numbers on your telephone: police, fire department, your doctor, the person you are to call in an emergency.

But when I am afraid, I will trust in you.
(Psalm 56:3)

Five

The Doorknocker

The Stranger's Strategy

A child molester looks for a child who is
home alone. He knows you are not
supposed to let strangers in. He tries to
make you think it is OK. Here are lies he
uses to trick you.

"My car broke down. I need to use your
telephone."

"Your mother asked me to fix the
furnace. It might explode. You must let
me fix it."

"I have a package for you. I can't leave it outside."

Your Protection Plan

Basic Rule: Never open the door for a stranger.

1. You hear a knock. Talk in a loud voice through the *closed* door. Ask, "Who is it?"

2. You do not know the person. Say, "My mother can't come to the door right now. Put your business card under the door. My mother will call you."

3. The stranger has a package. Say, "You can leave it at the door. Or come

back another time. I have to leave the door now. Good-bye."

4. The stranger hangs around outside. Call your parents or the police.

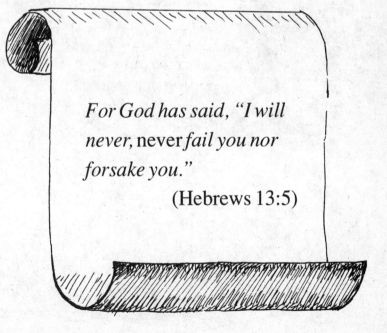

For God has said, "I will never, never fail you nor forsake you."
(Hebrews 13:5)

Six

Looking for
the Lost

The Stranger's Strategy

Sometime you might wander away from your family or friends. You cannot find your way back. You are lost.

The child molester looks for children who are lost. He knows how scary it feels. He hopes you will go with him.

Here are some things he will say:

"I'll help you look for your parents."

"Come on! I'll drive you home!"

"Let's buy some ice cream. We'll come back. By then, your parents will be here. They will wait for you."

Your Protection Plan

Basic Rule: Find the person in charge of the place where you are.

What to do if you get lost:
1. Do not go with anyone to look for your parents or the person who is taking care of you.

2. Think: Who is in charge here? A salesperson? An usher? A lifeguard? A policeman? Tell that person you are lost.

3. Stay with the person in charge. Let someone else page or look for your parents.

How to keep from getting lost:

1. Don't wander off alone in public places.

2. Always tell the person in charge of you where you'll be. Do not go anywhere else.

3. In wooded places, always go with friends. Mark a trail by tying yarn on trees. Follow the yarn trail home.

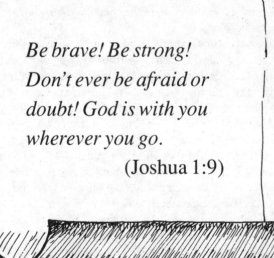

Be brave! Be strong! Don't ever be afraid or doubt! God is with you wherever you go.
(Joshua 1:9)

A Note to Parents

Crimes against children abound. It is not enough to say to a child, "Don't talk to strangers," or "Don't go with strangers." Outsmarting a clever sex offender is beyond a child's ability.

What is needed is a protection plan. Knowledge and a plan of action provide the best possible means of escaping an encounter unharmed.

As parents, we would like to spare our children anxiety by avoiding the topic. But, unfortunately, safety is incompatible with naiveté. We need to let our children know that there are unbalanced people who prey on children.

How we tell them is important. We don't want to cause playground paranoia or housebound horrors. But we do want them to have a healthy fear of the child molester—a fear that produces wise caution.

As soon as our children can understand, we teach them that their personal safety is their responsibility. We teach them respect for electricity, fire, and knives. We show them how to cross the street and how to approach dogs. We provide swimming lessons.

In the same way, we need to prepare our children for a possible confrontation with a child molester. Not to do so leaves them vulnerable to attack, injury, molestation, rape, or murder.

Together, you and your child can read about the tricks that child molesters use to induce children into going with them. You will want to discuss each threatening situation with your child. Then plan some responses designed to help your child avoid becoming a victim. As you look at the suggested responses, alter or add to them so they fit your personal requirements.

A child of preschool age won't require the same amount of information about protective measures as an older child who is home alone or outside unsupervised for any length of time. Start the little one with the basic rules and add more information as he becomes able to handle more responsibility. Don't say it once and think that you've done your duty. Check on your child from time to time to see what he remembers.

Make Learning Fun

Role playing can help make learning fun. Let your child play the stranger and you, as the child, model the right responses. Switch roles and observe what your child says and does as he portrays the child.

As your youngster comes to understand how to handle each threatening situation, his growing self-confidence should put fear in proper perspective. Role playing will give your child practice in performance that one day may save his life.

Another activity you might want to suggest to your child is to draw pictures of children responding in safe ways to the stranger's tricks.

The quiz on page 45 provides an opportunity to reemphasize vital information.

Additional Helps

Some neighborhoods provide block parents or safe houses identified by large signs in their windows. These homes are safety approved by the police and are available to children facing emergencies. If your area doesn't have a safe house, you might want to establish one.

For the rare time you might need to send a stranger for your child, agree on a secret password known only to your family. If the stranger knows the word, your child will know that you have sent him.

Preventing and Dealing with Lostness

A lost child is a frightened child. He is vulnerable to those who prey on children. Preventive habits offer the best protection.

43

Never leave a child alone in a car or a toy department while you shop elsewhere. Your child should not wander beyond the point where you can see each other.

Provide your child with an identification bracelet showing his name, address, phone number, and doctor's number. In a panic it's easy to forget basic information.

Instruct your child in the use of a telephone. Tie coins in the corner of a handkerchief and pin it inside a pocket in case he needs to use a public phone.

Plan with your child what you will do if you ever become separated. Both of you should report to the local police who can then put you in touch with each other. If your child goes to the person in charge of the area where's he lost, that person can call the police. Otherwise he'll probably need to use a public telephone.

Emphasize the buddy system for outdoor excursions to the pond for pollywogs or to the woods for berries.

The child who is taught to trust the Lord knows the blessing of guidance and protection. In a time of crisis, he will lack fear and experience a clarity of thought that enables him to recall and put into action the protection plan that you have diligently worked out together. In addition, your child's faith activates the intervention of God, who is an ever present help in trouble.

Do You Remember?

Choose one word to go in each blank space below. Fill in the blanks. Then turn the page upside down to check your answers.

coins	in charge	different
strategy	tricks	go
know	dangerous	friendly
pocket	go	alone
alone	ID bracelet	strangers
wander	door	signs
child molesters	stranger	home
adults	in charge	

1. A stranger is a person I do not _____.

2. Some strangers are _____. They are called _____ _____ .

3. Child molesters look for children who are _____.

4. A dangerous stranger doesn't look _____ from other people.

5. A dangerous stranger acts _____ because he wants me to trust him.

6. The dangerous stranger has a _____. He uses it to make me go with him.

7. The dangerous stranger uses _____ to fool children.

8. Children should always be where someone is _____ _____.

9. Safe houses have _____ in their windows.

10. It's a good idea to put _____ in a handkerchief. I can carry them in my _____.

11. It's a good idea to wear an _____ _____.

12. On the playground, know who is

_____   _____ .

13. At home, don't open the _____
to _____ .

14. On the phone, don't tell strangers
that _____ are not at

_____ .

15. Out-of-doors, I should never _____
off _____ .

16. Someone in a car offers me a ride. I
don't _____ with him.

17. If I am lost, I do not ____ with
a _____ .

47